CONTENTS

In the Saddle

for the Saddlers

Best Wishes
Tony Davis 06,

Every good wish
Geoff Allen
Club Historian.

Geoffrey Bevan

by

A. R. Davis

ISBN

1 899316 33 7

Published by A. R. Davis
2006

Printed in Scotland by Solway Offset the Printers,
Heathhall Industrial Estate, Heathhall. Dumfries. DG1 3PQ.

ABOUT THE AUTHOR

Born in Kidderminster Worcestershire on the 28th October 1944. He lived and spent all his childhood on a council estate at Coalpool, Walsall, West Midlands, where he has many fond memories of playing football until dusk in the field along side Rushall Level Crossing on the Walsall to Lichfield Railway Line (pre Beeching), and showing off his skills to the passengers on the train as it was halted by the signal, before usually going home very dirty. He also took personal delight in beating the trolley bus, as he saw it encounter Harden Road Island from the Gully at the top of Warner Road and running down the hill to the Whateley Road bus stop (about 200 yards), where the fare was cheaper.

Since retiring after 35 years in industry in 2003, the author now resides in Castle Douglas in the beautiful area of Dumfries and Galloway in South West Scotland, and this has given him the opportunity to put pen to paper and write this short story of a cycle ride that he made to Liverpool in 1961.

His passion and enthusiasm for sport and in particular football becomes evident as the story unfolds and in fact he his still actively refereeing and proudly registered with the Scottish F.A. after previously being registered with Walsall F.A. and Staffordshire F.A. from whom he received their Long Service Awards.

This passion is only surpassed by his love for his lovely wife of over 40 years Christine and their children Mark and Andrea, who both still reside in Staffordshire.

From that significant day when he was taken at the age of 8 years 11 months on Saturday 19.9.53 to Fellows Park, Walsall for the first time by his Uncle Harold and Grand-dad Davis, his love for the beautiful game commenced, and his ingrained feelings for his home town club developed.

The fitness required to make the cycle ride, clearly started from the emphasis placed on sport in the senior schools at the time. Unfortunately in these modern times with so many other distractions, sport as he used to know it at school, with particular reference to Athletics, Basketball, Cricket, and Football is not pursued with the same energies and competitive edge even if your skills were limited, and it is to this end that he hopes readers will be encouraged to participate in some form of fitness activity in which they are comfortable, rather than being a couch potato or visual screen addict.

His love for the game continues, not only with refereeing, but going along with the converted (his wife), and goodness she really does give the referees some stick when supporting Queen of the South in the Scottish League Division One, where they are season ticket holders. This gives rise to a good quiz question, 'Where do they play '? which very few people down south seem to know. The answer is Palmerston Park, Dumfries.

It really is a wonderful weekend when a hat-trick of wins is achieved, but this has become quite rare of late. However he has now got past the stage of the game being the be all and end all of life when watching Walsall F.C. has taken him to the top of the mountain and then brought him back down with an almighty bump.

FOREWORD

There would be very few 'Saddlers' fans who would dispute the glory years for Walsall F.C. coincided with the Bill Moore Era, and in particular their first ever season in the old Division Two, Season 1961/62, and what is now the Coca-Cola Championship.

The story features their first visit to Anfield in a league match, the home of a resurgent Liverpool F.C. and with new manager Bill Shankly at the helm, who would go on to win promotion as champions that season to Division One, and have had an illustrious history ever since.

As fans of that era Tony and his friend Geoffrey set off on a long distance cycle ride in support of their heroes, a feat which is to be commended for two lads of 16yrs and 15yrs respectively. It was also done with the minimum of fuss and which did not get to the ears of the players at that time, and who would have embraced such support if they had known.

Tony recalls what it was like at the time in a funny, light- hearted story, including additional factual information, which should appeal to a wide range of 'Saddlers' fans and one that I can heartily recommend.

Those of us lucky enough to play professional football realise the importance of such stories and memories of the fans in adding further chapters to the clubs history.

Keith Ball

ACKNOWLEDGMENTS

To Christine, my wife for all her support and patience in my pursuit of the information required for the story and constant encouragement, even after initial setbacks.

To my mother, without whom none of this would be possible.

To good friend Geoffrey for his comradeship, enthusiasm and recollections on such an eventful cycle ride.

On the technical side my brother Dennis for setting me up with the computer, and giving me advice.

Bernard and Pauline, Castle Douglas community IT centre.

The reproduction of match reports, photographs, and cartoon's is by kind permission of:
The Birmingham Post & Mail
The Liverpool Echo
The Walsall Observer
Walsall historian Geoff Allman
Andrew Poole at Walsall FC

Liverpool and England star Alan A'Court, who featured in both games against Walsall for his help and understanding plus supplying valuable material.

Keith Ball who's encouragement and patience is unrivalled in supplying information by post, the telephone, and at his home, where his lovely wife Marie's hospitality made our chats that more enjoyable.

I would also like to thank the following for their time, knowledge and help in making the writing of the story such an enjoyable experience for me:

Ken Hodgkisson, Albert McPherson, George Meek, Grenville Palin, and special thanks to friends Brian, Steve, Terry, Dave, Alistair, Allan, Hilda, and Dave Atherton.

Solway Offset for their advice on publishing and making it look easy and the finished article look so impressive.

Apologies in advance, as to the views expressed and comments passed are strictly the authors only.

Chapter One

EARLY DAYS

I had always enjoyed the excitement of travelling the country, stopping off at all the interesting towns, and wishing to quantify and pinpoint their locations. This would invariably incorporate finding the football grounds and having a look around. Funnily enough I never had a problem remembering the names of all ninety two league club grounds, although I think it would be more difficult now with all the new stadiums that have been built and new names given.

The travelling started when I purchased my first bicycle a blue Raleigh Trent Sports which had a three speed Sturmy Archer gear and weighed 42lbs, and with a loaded saddle bag 63lbs.

I brought the bicycle from a cycle shop in Lichfield Street, Walsall with a deposit of £5 and then by regular payments on an instalment card, over 52 weeks. The cycle cost £20, 15 shillings and 10 pennies (£20.75pence). My dad and brother came along with me to see the bicycle before the deal was done. To obtain the cycle I had to save my paper round money. Mr Tommy Gould worked at the Express & Star offices in Station Street, Walsall and was responsible for the distribution of the 'Stars' in North Walsall and lived in the same street as I did, consequently I became his No 1 paper kid, which entailed a morning round delivering the national daily newspapers to Goscote Estate before school and a evening round after school, distributing 7 dozen Express & Stars on the Rivers Estate, plus selling outside the Elkington factory when the workers came out, before finally cashing up at his house when you had finished. Saturdays entailed doing the evening round again to sell 'The Sporting Star' (Football Final), and then standing outside the Gaumont cinema on the bridge (now a Tesco store), to sell yet more 'Stars', finally catching the trolley bus and getting home to Mrs Gould's around 9 o'clock, where Mrs Gould had cooked her husband and me steak (privileged eh!). Sunday's entailed collecting all the money in from the customers and taking the change to the landlord at the 'Harden Pub', all this added up to a weekly income of 15 shillings (180 old pennies or 75 new pence).

This sense of adventure really took off in 1960 when I became a member of the Youth Hostels Association, for which your parent had to give consent being under the age of 16 yrs.

I had struck up a good friendship in those days with a schoolmate at the Joseph Leckie Grammar and Secondary Modern School, The Delves, Walsall (No problems in those days of pupils getting on with one another), and it was a big school. His name was Paul (Dougal) Collins and he lived at the posh end of town on the Park Hall Estate, Birmingham Rd.

This unlikely friendship had started when we had both just gone to The Leckie age 11 yrs, when we offered each other out over some trivial disagreement, probably to get self-esteem in our class. The scrap took place after lessons on waste ground behind the school and near to a brook. With classmates in attendance it was some fight, and we both got very dirty, (Our new grey blazers with maroon edging and caps to match took a particular drubbing). Dougal' won fair and square, but I was not disgraced and we became firm friends from that day on. Little did we know that four years later into our friendship that we would do a cycle tour of the Lake District in our school holidays, and this we did by pre – booking the various youth hostels in advance.

Chapter Two

HOW IT ALL BEGAN

I have supported Walsall F.C. for over 50 years. They are affectionately known to their supporters under the nickname "The Saddlers" derived from the fact of the town being famous for it's leather and saddle industry, (saddles having been made for her majesty the Queen).

It all began during season 1953-54 "The Saddlers" were in the old Division 3(South). It was the tenth league game of the season and this had yielded seven defeats and three draws, and was to be the third successive season they would finish bottom (24th position) and would have to apply for re-election, which in those days was down to the votes of the various league club chairmen at the Football Leagues Annual A.G.M., who invariably voted to keep Walsall F.C. in and the likes of non league Peterborough United (Posh) out. This was largely due to the votes of the other Midland chairmen (the said old palls act). On no fewer than seven occasions Walsall have had to seek re-election, since the last war.

My father (Dennis) was not really into football so it was agreed my Uncle Harold nicknamed "H" and my grand-dad Sydney Davis could take me along to my first ever football match aged 8 years 11 months at the old Fellows Park ground in Hillary St, Pleck, Walsall. The ground got its name as a tribute to many years of self-sacrificing work for the club by one of its former chairmen, local business man Mr H L Fellows in 1930.

Uncle Harold is now in his late seventies and still goes to all the home games, and a fair few away matches and must rank as one of their most ardent supporters enjoying and suffering all their highs and lows over the years, as well as being extremely knowledgeable about the game.

Fellows Park is now the site of a huge Morrison's Supermarket. (The last game to be played there was on the 1st of May 1990 versus Rotherham United). It was also the only ground with three sides in the Football League, for behind the railway end goals stood the Orgill Laundry, so there's a quiz question for you! At the laundry end there also stood a huge Half-Time scoreboard, similar in size to what you would see at a cricket ground, usually with big letters A through to

T. In the match day programme there would be a key. The first letters always corresponded to the games featuring Aston Villa, Wolverhampton Wanderers, Birmingham City, and West Bromwich Albion, also stating their opponents. When the half times were known the grounds-man would put the score up for example, A 0-1, B 1-1 etc. This would be the only way of keeping in touch with how your team were getting on, particularly if you were a Wolves fan visiting Walsall (Wolves and Villa were usually away when Walsall were at home). There were no loudspeaker announcements or Radio 5 Live to give the scores.

It was Saturday the 19th September 1953 and the attendance was 9,666 and Walsall were to achieve their first victory of the season thanks to a goal from Centre half No 5 Len Horne, who blasted home a free kick from fully 40 yards out by the right hand touch line, main stand side, (I was standing by the wall in a packed enclosure of the main stand, and can vividly recollect the moment, as the ball travelled like a cannonball, high into the laundry end goal).

My uncle said I was a lucky omen and consequently took me to most of the home games thereon.

Chapter Three

THE BILL MOORE ERA

The beginning of the clubs greatest ever period coincided with the appointment of Bill Moore as manager. He had earned great respect first as a trainer with Nott's County, who were managed by the former Aston Villa and England forward Eric Houghton and then when Houghton returned to Villa Park as manager, he took Bill with him as right hand man and he played a big part in Villa's FA Cup triumph over Manchester United in 1957.

In the December following that Wembley victory, Moore the "iron man" trainer was asked to take over from Jack Love as manager of Walsall who had been going through a difficult time and were in deep trouble at the foot of the Division 3 (South). In no time at all he rallied the team and re-election was avoided

Season 1958-59 was Bill's first full season in charge and saw the leagues restructured, the old Third Division South and North sections replaced by Divisions Three and Four, with Walsall playing in the Fourth. He was confident of success but the team had to settle for a creditable sixth place.

This moderate success, instead of the previous never ending battles against relegation gave the club new self belief which now had Bill in partnership with the added drive of new chairman Ernie Thomas, the barge builder who was appointed in 1958, plus the ongoing expertise, enthusiasm and quite efficiency of secretary Ernest Wilson. He also continued to be aided by the capable Vic Potts as first team trainer, who came with Bill from the 'Villa'.

Season 1959-60 ended with Walsall becoming 4th Division champions and getting into Division Three and finally giving their die- hard supporters something to cheer about.

Season 1960-61:The following article was printed in the Sports Argus by Tom Duckworth on February 18th 1961, which illustrates what an astute manager Bill Moore was.

Now, in his third full season with Walsall, he has licked what was a struggling outfit into shape and built them into a fit, confident and capable combination.

Money has never been plentiful, nor gates large, indeed there have been times when he has had to sell. But he has never weakened the team.

For instance when BRIAN TAYLOR was transferred to Birmingham City for £14,000, he replaced him with namesake Colin, obtained for a song from Stourbridge.

Today COLIN TAYLOR, with the dynamite left foot, is one of the most dangerous and sought after wingers in the game.

At the end of last season Bill replenished Walsall's bank balance again with the sale of right half PETER BILLINGHAM and reserve centre half STAN JONES to West Bromwich Albion for another £14,000.

Now, in local boy KEN HILL, he has developed another right half, who looks like being better than Billingham.

Bill Moore has used some of the money received from transfer fees to strengthen other positions and build up the side

There have been no goalkeeping worries since JOHN CHRISTIE was brought cheaply from Southampton. JIMMY DUDLEY, signed for £4,000 from West Bromwich Albion, added stability to the half back line.

TOMMY WILSON, centre forward of Nottingham Forest's Cup winning team, secured for a similar sum, has fitted in splendidly into the attack.

Bill Moore has also kept a close eye on the Midland "Big Four" for bargains. At the end of last season he snapped up GRANVILLE PALIN from Wolves for £2,000 and JOHN SHARPLES for a give away £200.

Following injuries to first team full back HARRY HADDINGTON and BILL GUTTRIDGE, Palin and Sharples have done so well they will be hard to displace.

And young TREVOR FOSTER-"Keep an eye on this lad, " says Bill-he has shown great promise at inside and outside left when called upon.

But Walsall do not intend of selling fine young prospects like Hill, Taylor, and Foster.

A lot will depend upon attendances, which have kept pretty steady around last season's level of 10,000 to 11,000.

"Gates could be better", admits Bill, "But considering the all-round drop throughout the country, our fans have stuck to us pretty well."

How will the fans react if Walsall win promotion?

Would they roll up to see big name clubs like Sunderland, Liverpool and Preston?

It would need a bigger build-up on Walsall's part.

"My aim is a pool of 17 or 18 players that can be thoroughly relied on for first team duty, and the rest promising youngsters," says Moore.

Promotion had always been a possibility but it was when Walsall beat Bury twice at Christmas that it became a very real chance:

On Saturday 23rd December 1960, at home in front of an attendance of 10,702 a 1-0 victory was secured with a brave diving header off Tony Richards, this was followed up on Boxing Day with a remarkable 4-3 away victory at Gigg Lane, Bury with an attendance off 13,102. In front of considerable away support Walsall had raced into a 4-0 half time lead with a faultless display, only to be pegged back in the second half, and left hanging on for the final whistle. The first half goals were scored by, Hodgkisson, Wilson, Richards, and Taylor.

The two games at Christmas were pulsating affairs and I was fortunate to attend both.

Eventually Season 1960-61 ended with this truly exciting side still achieving further honours by becoming runners up to Bury and being promoted to Division 2.

This was achieved with a 2-1 win with goals from "Cannonball" Colin Taylor (4mins) and Colin Askey (56mins) on a truly memorable Wednesday evening, April 26th 1961 against local rivals Shrewsbury Town at the Gay Meadow, who included in their side the legendry Arthur Rowley. A new record club attendance of 18,971 was set and still stands to the present day, and on the night Rowley scored the equaliser on 44mins from a disputed penalty,thus claiming his 379th League goal to equal the record held at the time by Dixie Dean. He went on to score 434 League goals-a record which still stands today. It was pandemonium as the news came through that our nearest challengers Queens Park Rangers, had lost at Reading, all the Walsall supporters were ecstatic, dancing and hugging with complete strangers on the pitch at the end of the match.

SHREWSBURY TOWN FOOTBALL CLUB LTD.

GAY MEADOW
PHONE 6068

OFFICIAL PROGRAMME 6d.

No. 46. WALSALL THIRD DIVISION. Wednesday, April 26th, 1961

2749

HAIL AND FAREWELL!

It is our pleasure this evening to welcome to the Gay Meadow the Walsall team, its Directors and Officials along with a host of keen and loyal Supporters. To all of them we say "well done" and yet we must stress that our warm friendship does not extend to charity, tonight you will find that our team and Supporters are as keen to win this match as much, and more than, any other in the season.

Again to Walsall we say if you do go up to the Second Division our sincerest congratulations will go to you and we know your hope will be that we join you in the near future.

Now to our own affairs, we are confident that no real Supporter will grumble at our efforts this season, we had our best F.A. Cup effort for a long time, reached the semi-final of the League Cup, and have almost ensured ourselves of a place in the top half of the table. Our record shows we have beaten most of the leading Clubs, so here again beware Walsall, we mean to improve even further that proud record. Naturally to top the Season off we look forward to Arthur Rowley attaining his magnificent and richly earned record in goal scoring.

To all of you who have supported, contributed, played, worked or officiated in any way, thank you indeed for your efforts in the 1960/61 season.

SEASON TICKETS.

Enquiries are plentiful and most encouraging, if you are interested call at the Club Office, where we will be delighted to let you have an application form for next season.

Cheerio until next season but we do ask you during the close season not to relax your efforts on our behalf, we will still be working hard to progress and please you.

The evening had been fantastic from the off with all available coaches, namely Central (Co-op travel) and Dawsons being commandeered for the short journey of 30 miles along the A 5 (no M 54 in those days). What a never to be forgotten sight that cavalcade was, solid traffic all the back to Wellington.

So there you have it little Walsall were in Division Two, after an absence of 60 years after not very long ago being the Cinderella club, seeking re-election so often it was a joke, but not any more. They would now be taking on the likes of Newcastle United, Sunderland, Derby County and a Liverpool side being rebuilt by the great Bill Shankley.

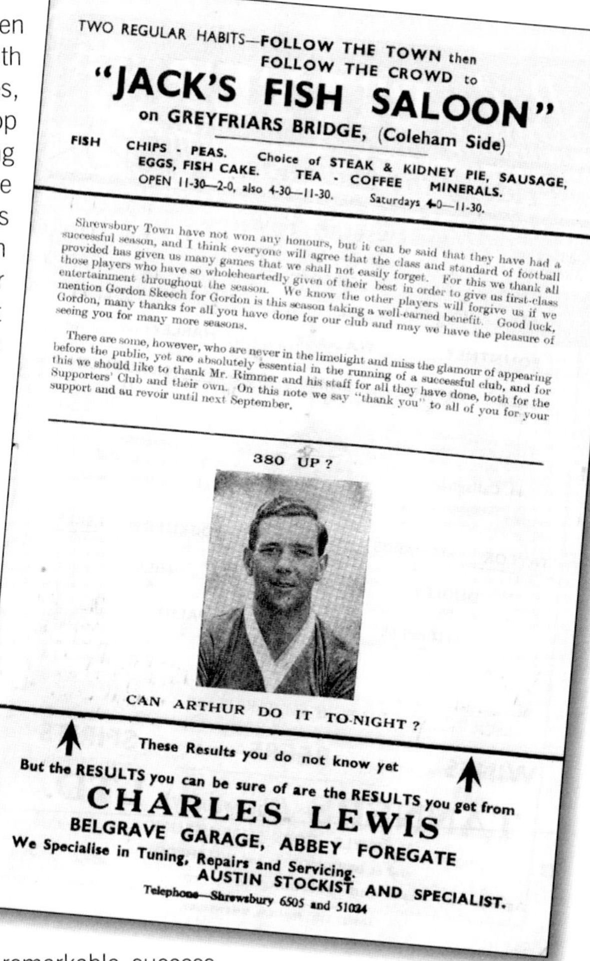

TWO REGULAR HABITS—FOLLOW THE TOWN then FOLLOW THE CROWD to
"JACK'S FISH SALOON"
on GREYFRIARS BRIDGE, (Coleham Side)
FISH CHIPS - PEAS. Choice of STEAK & KIDNEY PIE, SAUSAGE, EGGS, FISH CAKE. TEA - COFFEE MINERALS.
OPEN 11-30—2-0, also 4-30—11-30. Saturdays 4-0—11-30.

Shrewsbury Town have not won any honours, but it can be said that they have had a
successful season, and I think everyone will agree that the class and standard of football
provided has given us many games that we shall not easily forget. For this we thank all
those players who have so wholeheartedly given of their best in order to give us first-class
entertainment throughout the season. We know the other players will forgive us if we
mention Gordon Skeech for Gordon is this season taking a well-earned benefit. Good luck,
Gordon, many thanks for all you have done for our club and may we have the pleasure of
seeing you for many more seasons.

There are some, however, who are never in the limelight and miss the glamour of appearing
before the public, yet are absolutely essential in the running of a successful club, and for
this we should like to thank Mr. Rimmer and his staff for all they have done, both for the
Supporters' Club and their own. On this note we say "thank you" to all of you for your
support and au revoir until next September.

380 UP ?

CAN ARTHUR DO IT TO-NIGHT ?

These Results you do not know yet
But the RESULTS you can be sure of are the RESULTS you get from
CHARLES LEWIS
BELGRAVE GARAGE, ABBEY FOREGATE
We Specialise in Tuning, Repairs and Servicing.
AUSTIN STOCKIST AND SPECIALIST.
Telephone—Shrewsbury 6505 and 51034

Bill Moore had achieved remarkable success in his first job as manager in securing successive promotions for Walsall, who were having the greatest period in their history. It also coincided with their best seasonal average home attendances.

59-60 12.045 60-61 10.670 61-62 12711

The record crowd for Fellows Park was also smashed on the night game in Division Two, 29th August 1961 versus Newcastle United. This was the second home game after clinching promotion with an attendance of 24,453 packed in, with no crowd trouble, many more locked out, and lots more having great difficulty to see. I was perched on the toilet block at the Hillary street end in the corner it was just a breeze block pee corner about seven / eight feet high, an excellent vantage point, mind you had to be careful with the wall the one side or else you would be out of the ground and down the railway embankment, some drop! The result by the way was a 1-0 home win with a truly tremendous goal from Billy Younger, when he whipped in a remarkable swerving shot from fully 30 yards after 28 minutes.

This attendance beat the previous record by nearly 4,000, which was 21,811 for a third round FA Cup-tie with Port Vale in 1956, where I was privileged to witness a terrific performance by Vale's England 'B' goalkeeper Ray King, Walsall losing the tie by 1-0.

The opening game on Saturday 19th August 1961 against Sunderland was an all ticket affair with 22,000 tickets available, but the attendance on the day was a little disappointing with only 18,420 there to see a Tony Richards hat-trick and a Tommy Wilson goal secure victory 4-3 in a topsy- turvy game, which included a goal for the visitors by the legendry Brian Clough, who was making his debut.

This was followed by a 1-0 defeat when visiting Newcastle United, but three days latter we were 3-1 winners against Derby County. The return fixture with Newcastle United saw Walsall turn the tables and win 1-0 and create the new attendance record.

A home game with Leyton Orient followed, and proved a big disappointment, for Manager Johnny Carey's team won 5-1.

Walsall picked up quickly, however, by drawing 1-1 with Southampton and beating Preston North End 3-2, both away games. A visit from Plymouth Argyle saw Walsall victorious1-0, after which Southampton made amends for dropping a point at the Dell by winning the return at Fellows Park 2-0. Swansea were the next team to get rewarded when they drew 0-0 at Walsall.

THE WALSALL FOOTBALL CLUB LTD.
FELLOWS PARK, WALSALL
№ 78
FOOTBALL LEAGUE 2nd DIVISION MATCH
WALSALL v SUNDERLAND
SATURDAY, 19th AUGUST, 1961.
KICK OFF 3 p.m.
GROUND (Schoolboy) 1/3
THIS TICKET IS ISSUED SUBJECT TO THE RULES AND REGULATIONS OF THE FOOTBALL ASSOCIATION AND THE FOOTBALL LEAGUE
THIS PORTION TO BE RETAINED
Secretary

Walsall then registered their most convincing victory of the season by beating Rotherham United 5-0 at Fellows Park.

Chapter Four

COACH OR CYCLE

Newly promoted from Division 3, and after making a promising start to the Season 1961-62,the first twelve games having yielded 14 points: won 6 lost 4 and drawn 2,Walsall were about to take on the favourites for the championship a Liverpool side being rebuilt by Bill Shankley.

Having already had my appetite wetted by seeing The Saddlers beat the likes of Sunderland, Derby County, and Newcastle United I decided to go to Liverpool on my bicycle which was still the same Raleigh Trent Sports, with a three speed Sturmy Archer gear, complete with saddle bag, which I brought with my paper money; even though there were numerous supporters travelling by coach with Central Co-op Travel, and Dawsons coaches, which involved taking in the match and then going on to Blackpool Illuminations. The cost for the coach at

the time was adults eleven shillings (55 pence) and children seven shillings and six pence (37 pence), compare that with to-day's prices and it would not get you into town on a bus or buy a cup of tea. It never entered my head to go by any other means because you simply did not have the money, being from a working class family with two younger sisters Suzanne and Anne and a younger brother Dennis, living on a council estate at Coalpool in Walsall.

Having already recently returned from a youth hostel cycle tour of Devon & Cornwall, as recently as the 10.08.61, taking in eleven youth hostels en route and amassing a total of 680 miles over a period of twelve days, with distances usually around 50 miles per day being cycled it did not appear to present a problem. The last day being the biggest stage from Shepton Mallet in Somerset to home at Warner Road, Coalpool, Walsall, Staffs, or as is now in the West Midlands, a total of 130 miles or more correctly 120 miles, because me and another friend Alan did the last 10 miles by train from Birmingham because we had enough being the end of the tour and all that and having been on the road all day since leaving Croscombe youth hostel near Wells at a quarter past nine in the morning on a breakfast of porridge, scrambled egg, bread and jam and a cup of tea. The duty for the day by the way for any seasoned youth hostel addicts of yesteryear was washing cooking utensils and dishes after breakfast, all this for ten shillings (50 new pence per night).

As you can see, there was no time for girls and any way they were pretty toffee nosed, as I was off the council estate and all that, whilst they all lived at the posh end of town, namely Birmingham Road, Broadway, or Park Hall.

I was a fit skinny youth of 16 years of age just having left Joseph Leckie grammar school The Delves Walsall with no "O" Levels, but 4 school certificates in English Literature,Geography,Art,&Physics with Chemistry. This meant academically if I had tried a little harder and achieved a further 5%, they would have been "O" Level passes; so there's a lesson for all you younger ones out there, although I did achieve success with further education in later years. I lived for sport representing the school teams at Athletics, Cricket & Football and I was also a member of Tipton Harriers, who had signed me up after a brilliant cross- country performance for the school in Victoria Park Tipton. It seemed like I was joining Liverpool F.C at the time.

I lived in Warner Rd, Coalpool, and was friendly with Geoffrey "Tubby" Bevan, don't ask me why he was called "Tubby" more likely chubby I'd say.

Tubby was really a friend of my brother Dennis and lived round the corner in Clare Rd, 200 yards away and had a good cycle also and when I mentioned the idea of going to Liverpool on our bikes he never gave it a second thought and I knew he liked cycling. He didn't go to Walsall's home games as regularly as me, but he still had his hometown team at heart.

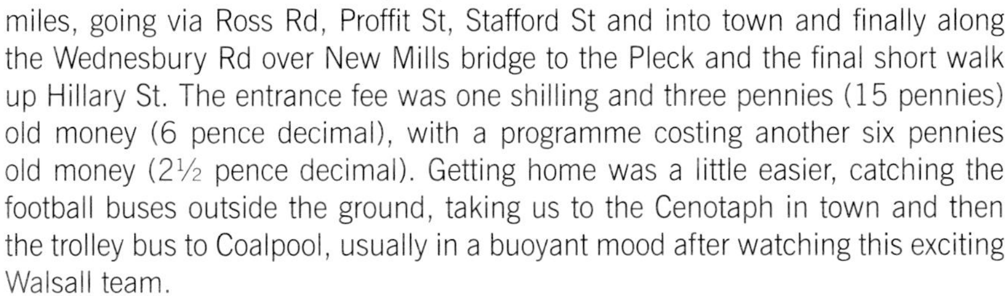

Home games at Fellows Park meant walking the entire distance from Coalpool, about five miles, going via Ross Rd, Proffit St, Stafford St and into town and finally along the Wednesbury Rd over New Mills bridge to the Pleck and the final short walk up Hillary St. The entrance fee was one shilling and three pennies (15 pennies) old money (6 pence decimal), with a programme costing another six pennies old money (2½ pence decimal). Getting home was a little easier, catching the football buses outside the ground, taking us to the Cenotaph in town and then the trolley bus to Coalpool, usually in a buoyant mood after watching this exciting Walsall team.

The line-up usually picked it-self with only 15 players being used in the first half of the season including our reserve goalkeeper.

This is surely testimony to the player's fitness of this era, as there were no substitutes either. The kit, boots, and footballs (nick-named "cassie") with its leather lace were all heavier, but may-be the standard leather boots with their ankle protection, fixed studs, and a thick leather strap across the middle plus solid toecaps were more conducive to the game than the modern synthetic material slipper footwear players now wear, and has given rise to an alarming number of broken bones in the foot of which there are 26, 14 of these form the toes, 5 are the notorious Metatarsal Bones joining the toes to the heel, and the other 7 make up the heel and back part of the foot. Admittedly when the "cassie" got soaked the players were glad of the extra protection. With today's sophisticated medical equipment, I find it strange why so many of today's footballers cry off games with the most minor of injuries, I know there are more games, but we also have the squad rotation system!

I used to watch the training at Pleck Park in the August school holidays, where football practice and small-sided games were carried out, there I stood and watched in awe my heros training. Training also took place at the nearby Walsall Golf Club on the Broadway, also back at Fellows Park there was a punch ball under the main stand and a small 'breeze block' built building nearby which was a weights room/ gymnasium for the players to train in. I recollect it was built when Ernie Thomas arrived as chairman, maybe because he owned a 'breeze block' manufacturing site ! They would also go out for long road runs.

After the training sessions I would hang around at the ground whilst they got changed and then obtain their autographs. After one such wait I still remember Colin Askey, all on his own, using the weights in the gymnasium to strengthen his knee muscles after a cartilage operation. If treatment was required for physiotherapy or more investigation was needed the players ended up going via the back door and jumping the queue at the old General Hospital in Wednesbury Road.

Chapter Five

IN THE SADDLE FOR THE "SADDLER'S.

Liverpool FC versus Walsall FC
Football League Division 2

Saturday 14.10.61,the weather was a cold damp misty morning and dawn was just breaking as myself with the nicknames of (Smiler or Speedy Davis), called at my friend Geoffrey (Tubby) Bevan's house at five thirty in the morning to begin what was to become an unforgettable journey on our bicycles.

Before we continue the tale I know you are wondering how on earth did I get those nick-names. Smiler was a nickname attributed to me by Bert, a teacher who taught German at the Joseph Leckie Grammar School. Well he was an excellent teacher for the subject, beard and all, but I did have this stupid little cough and usually disrupted the class, needless to say whenever Bert turned around from the blackboard he found me smiling, however the laugh was soon was on the other foot as I was usually put into detention after school or sent to see the deputy head Mr Joe Sturrock for lashings of the taws across my backside. He had a glass eye, and I'm sure this would account for him missing your buttocks occasionally.

Speedy was given to me by my senior team-mates at Tipton Harriers (notably Alan Whittle) who was a constant source of encouragement as I did fast times as a youth, particularly over the short legs in road relays (2-3 miles), the seniors doing the longer legs, and a little later I became Staffordshire Youth Cross Country Champion in 1962.

Tubby and I were both dressed similarly, trousers, black school shoes and myself in black PVC Bomber jacket, with Tubby wearing a short suede jacket, which the night before had a broken zip, causing him to cut the duffels off his duffel coat and sew them onto the jacket. His mother must have thought, 'I wonder what Geoffrey is up to!', because she had told him he could not go to Liverpool. As the day progressed it was to be proven that we were very much underdressed for such a journey.

Geoffrey's bike was also a Raleigh, albeit an old one, hand painted dark blue, with silver lugs and a fixed cog and a dodgy front ripped tyre, which he had patched up with another small piece of tyre on the inner rim; he also had a saddlebag.

With Tubby out in front, it was necessary for us both to have our Every Ready battery cycle lamps on, front and rear for a short while as it was still dark and quite foggy as we made our way along the familiar surroundings of Goscote and Lower Farm Bloxwich, pedalling in earnest along the A34 through Great Wyrley and onto Cannock, then past Littleton Colliery, continuing and making good time to Stafford. With the mist still evident in the surrounding fields we continued towards Stone, however it started to clear when we approached the built up area of Newcastle under Lyme. As we started to climb out by the Bus Station we decided it was the appropriate place to make our first stop for the toilets and refreshments namely water and a packet of biscuits. Great Eh! All with the hullabaloo of the people and the buses busily pulling in and out.

Continuing along the A34 we fervently got pedalling again and continued our climb out of Newcastle and around the edge of Stoke on Trent until we picked up the A50 around Alsager, then hitting the open fields again, heading towards Holmes Chapel. We really were moving along quite famously and a further short stretch and the open road saw us pass through Knutsford and towards the signs pointing the way to Warrington, which was a longer stretch. With no real signs of genuine fatigue, only excitement has we homed in on our destination, and certainly with no thoughts of having to do the return journey. As we approached Warrington, and over the swing bridge which crosses the Manchester ship canal at Grappenhall we encountered a traffic jam but just zoomed along on the outside, bear in mind Tubby had to be more careful because of the fixed cog on his bike and couldn't stop pedalling, he already clipped the kerb once when forgetting and trying to freewheel and nearly fell off his bike. We then proceeded to cross the River Mersey near Warrington town centre and headed out on the A57 towards Liverpool, until arriving at the suburb of Dovecot were the road became a duel carriageway and at one of the traffic light junctions there was various shops, including a fish and chip shop and a bakers shop.

Upon seeing the fish and chip shop was open and feeling rather hungry after our arduous bike ride, we both went in and purchased a bag of chips each. Whilst standing in the queue, we experienced our first taste of the friendly open-ness of the local Liverpool people who were pulling our legs about our "Brummie" accents", when we had enquired of them the direction of the football ground. After a little friendly banter they duly pointed us in the direction of Anfield. We exited the shop and called at the adjoining bakers shop and purchased an uncut loaf of bread. We broke the loaf in half, hollowed out the insides and filled them with chips.

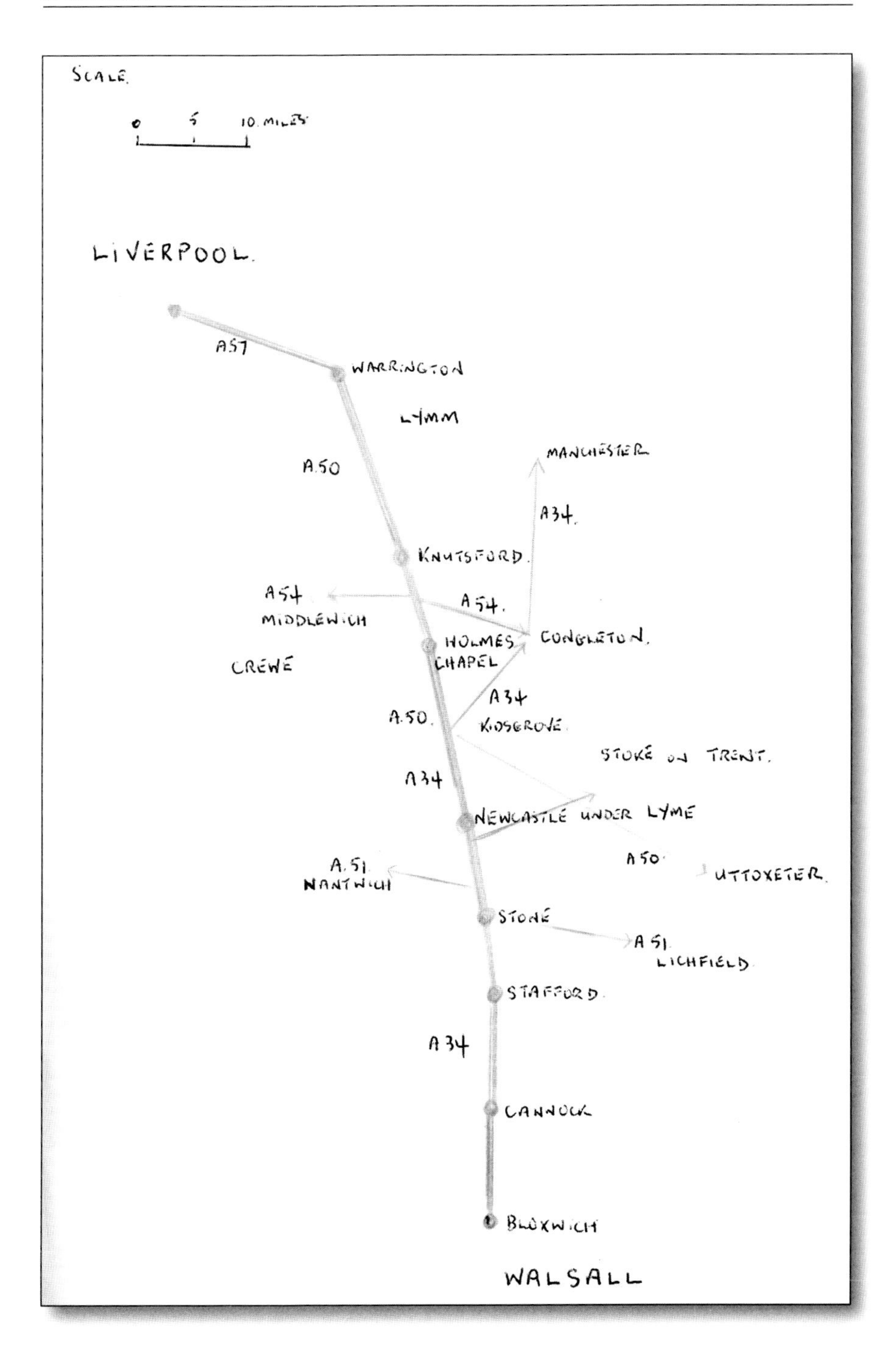
SCALE.
0 5 10 MILES
LIVERPOOL.
A57
WARRINGTON
LYMM
A.50
MANCHESTER
A34.
KNUTSFORD.
A54
MIDDLEWICH
A54.
HOLMES CHAPEL
CONGLETON.
CREWE
A34
A.50.
KIDSGROVE.
STOKE ON TRENT.
A34
NEWCASTLE UNDER LYME
A.51
NANTWICH
A50
UTTOXETER.
STONE
A51
LICHFIELD.
STAFFORD.
A34
CANNOCK
BLOXWICH
WALSALL

We stood outside the shop eating our bread and chips, with a feeling of pride and a justified satisfaction of achieving our goal of cycling to Liverpool.

The following is a brief breakdown of the journey.

Home-Cannock-Stafford	A34	20miles	Depart 5.30am
Stafford-Stone	A34	7 miles	
Stone-Newcastle under Lyme	A34	9miles	Arrive 7.30am
Newcastle under Lyme-Holmes Chapel	A50	16miles	
Holmes Chapel-Knutsford	A50	8miles	
Knutsford-Warrington	A50	16miles	
Warrington-Liverpool	A57	16 miles	Arrive 12.00pm (Dovecot).

We arrived outside Anfield in good time for the 3.o'clock kick off and with time to spare, started looking for somewhere safe to leave our bikes while we were at the football match.

The local houses consisted of mainly Victorian terraced dwellings, with courtyards and basements all within a stone's throw of the football ground. They were very similar in appearance to those in the T.V. soap Coronation St, complete with a cat sitting on the yard wall.

One such row of houses was in Arkles Road, and so we decided to knock the door of one such property, and after a short delay were greeted by a very nice lady, who looked every bit like the film star Audrey Hepburn. She was wearing a pinny

over her dress and had a feather duster in her hand, and was somewhat surprised when confronted by two dishevelled teenagers with "Brummie" accents, asking if we could leave our bikes there for the duration of the game. " No problem lads, but it will cost you a three penny bit (just over one new pence), I will shut the front door and go and open the back yard gate, just go down the entry and you can leave your bikes quite safely in the yard". She enquired as to what had brought us to Liverpool, and we gave her a short resume of our little tale, which resulted in us putting our bikes to the front of the gates so that we could get away quickly after the game, for she was obviously expecting more bikes before the game. We duly thanked her, parked our bikes and said we should be back after the game around 5.o'clock. She asked our names and introduced herself as Mrs Metcalfe, so with a lovely smile and a cheery wave said, "Tara lads, enjoy the game and don't forget that you have left your bikes in Arkles Rd", in a posh Liverpool accent and closed the gate behind us.

We paid our entrance fee at the turnstile and entered onto the terraces at the Kemlyn Rd side of the ground, which had not really started to fill up, this enabled us to meet up with other Walsall supporters, who informed us that after the game they were continuing on to Blackpool for the illuminations to make a complete day of it. They listened to our story with admiration and a certain amount of disbelief as to why we had gone to such extreme lengths in support of the "Saddlers", one even suggested we had got there on motor bikes, however they obviously felt sorry for us, because they shared their butties and gave us a drink. They also gave us extra butties to eat on our journey home. We were positioned at the front of the terracing, near to the famous Kop end, and in those days the pitch was elevated by around three feet from the base, so you appeared to be at eye level for watching the game. As the kick off approached, the ground began to fill up with the local supporters who completely surrounded us. In those day's there was no segregation in the stands or on the terracing. We soon developed a friendly banter, which was to become more biased as the game progressed.

Chapter Six

THE MATCH OF THE DAY

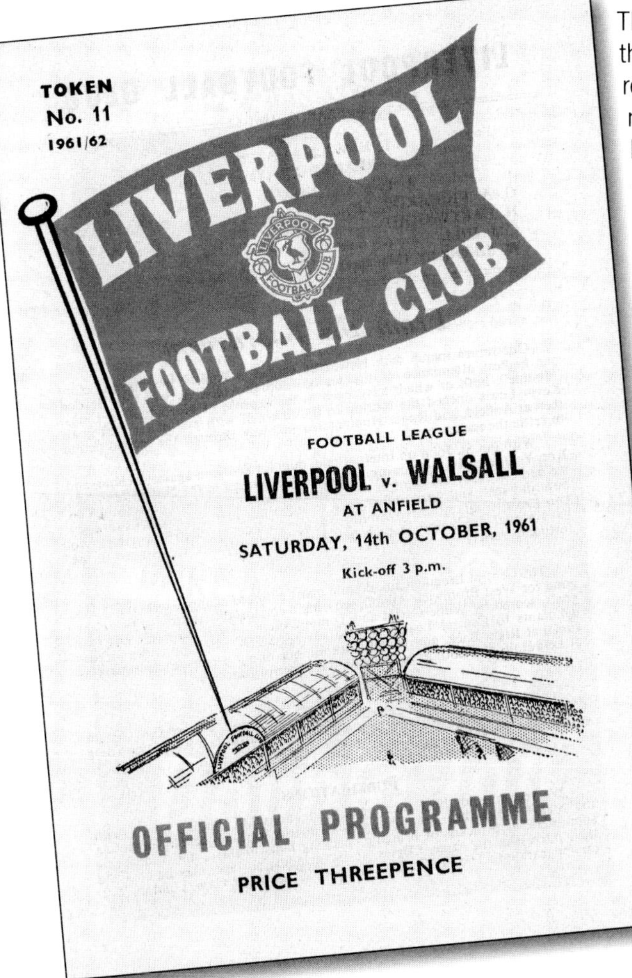

The Liverpool Echo gave the following pre-match report in the Friday night edition, by Leslie Edwards, which was also very amusing.

Don't under- estimate Walsall...

Little Walsall, who will be playing at Anfield to-morrow, have never met Liverpool in a league match. They were in the second division for some seasons prior to the turn of the century, but Liverpool missed them because they had gained promotion. The visiting side have a niche of their own. In their third division days they beat the mighty Arsenal in a never-to-be-forgotten Cup -tie. The ball they used that day (now deflated by time and looking more shrivelled than a prune) still has its place of honour in a glass case in the boardroom. It is one of the few links with the past. The other is the blank laundry wall at the one end of the ground a few feet from the dead-ball line. Visiting right- wingers can never make much speed down this wing for fear of flattening out (or being flattened out) against this barrier.

Like Liverpool, Walsall, have had some managers in their time. One of them sported a "bow tie" with shirt cuffs to match, and the bowler hat, which was part of a manager's uniform in the 20's and 30's. They say he used to keep a case of beer under his office desk. When the team had only one fit left winger and that player put two corner kicks "into the crowd" in a home match, the manager commanded the trainer to "put blocks on this fellow on Monday".

The trainer was mystified "What blocks", he asked.

Apparently no wooden blocks were available, so the manager said. "Get four bricks and place two of them on either side of the ball at the corner flag and make that fellow take corners until he knows how to keep the ball in play".

The bricks were placed and the winger started his punishing chore, and at the first time of asking connected nicely, not with the ball, but with two of the bricks.

He did not play again for some five weeks, and Walsall got along as best they could without a left- winger worthy of the name from that day.

Fixture Oddity

14.10.61

LEAGUE TABLES

Football League—Division II

	P.	W.	D.	L.	F.	A.	Pts.
Liverpool	12	10	1	1	31	6	21
Southampton	12	7	2	3	27	11	16
Leyton O.	12	6	2	4	23	13	14
Luton T.	12	7	0	5	30	24	14
Walsall	12	6	2	4	21	19	14
Derby C.	12	6	2	4	25	24	14
Rotherham U.	11	7	0	4	23	23	14
Huddersfield	12	5	3	4	21	19	13
Plymouth A.	12	5	3	4	17	19	13
Norwich	12	4	4	4	19	19	12
Sunderland	12	5	2	5	23	23	12
Swansea	12	3	6	3	22	26	12
Bury	12	6	0	6	16	23	12
Middlesbrough	11	4	3	4	21	19	11
Scunthorpe	12	4	3	5	26	25	11
Brighton	12	3	5	4	16	23	11
Newcastle U.	12	4	2	6	14	14	10
Preston N.E.	12	4	2	6	15	19	10
Stoke C.	12	3	3	6	18	20	9
Leeds U.	12	3	2	7	12	23	8
Bristol R.	12	3	1	8	14	21	7
Charlton A.	12	1	2	9	12	33	4

Central League

	P.	W.	D.	L.	F.	A.	Pts.
Aston Villa	12	11	0	1	32	12	22
Wolves	12	8	2	2	36	13	18
Liverpool	12	9	0	3	28	13	18
Manchester U	12	8	2	2	41	21	18
Burnley	11	8	1	2	30	12	17
Newcastle U.	12	8	1	3	28	19	17
Blackburn R.	11	6	2	3	30	16	14
Huddersfield T.	10	6	1	3	23	19	13
Blackpool	12	5	2	5	22	19	12
Derby Co.	12	6	0	6	26	27	12
Bolton W.	13	4	3	6	19	25	11
Manchester C.	11	4	2	5	22	29	10
Barnsley	11	4	2	5	19	32	10
Everton	11	4	1	6	15	19	9
Chesterfield	12	4	1	7	18	38	9
Sheffield U.	12	3	2	7	17	24	8
Sheffield W.	11	2	4	5	18	26	8
West Brom. A.	12	3	2	7	11	23	8
Bury	12	2	2	8	16	22	6
Leeds U.	11	3	0	8	16	30	6
Preston N.E.	11	1	2	8	16	23	4
Stoke City	11	1	2	8	6	27	4

Much is made of the fact that Liverpool have met and beaten Sunderland and Newcastle, teams expected to be among their most serious rivals. Look at the league table and you will discover that Liverpool have yet to meet all eight clubs who lie immediately below them!

Liverpool last met Walsall in a Cup- tie at Walsall. There were times when Liverpool looked like losing, but eventually Jack Halmer and company came along with a handsome win by some three or four goals if my memory serves. The Liverpool party were leaving the ground in their coach when some spectator speeded half back Bobby Paisley with a painful kick on the shin.

With St. John back and maybe Ronnie Yeats too, Liverpool should get back to winning after their luckless lapse at Middlesborough. But any team, which can beat Rotherham 5-0 is to be respected. It would be unwise to take too lightly the not-considerable repute of a side, which has spent most of its life in the Third Division.

The Birmingham Mail pre-match report concentrated on the team news which was, Liverpool At Full Strength

Walsall take wing–half Rawlings to Liverpool tomorrow in case Hill (injured Achilles tendon) is unfit, but manager Bill Moore said today he expected to field an unchanged team.

Yeats, Liverpool's £25,000 6ft Scottish centre-half came through a fitness test on an injured right shoulder today and returns to the team.

Yeats missed last Saturday's match at Middlesborough, which brought about Liverpool's first defeat.

Liverpool now revert, to the team which took 21 points out of the first 22 possible. White the captain is able to return to right-back having been the stand–in for Yeats at Middlesborough where White twice put through his own goal.

Ian St. John, £37,500 Scottish international centre-forward returns from international duties to resume the leadership in place of Arrowsmith.

PEN PICTURE'S of the LIVERPOOL TEAM

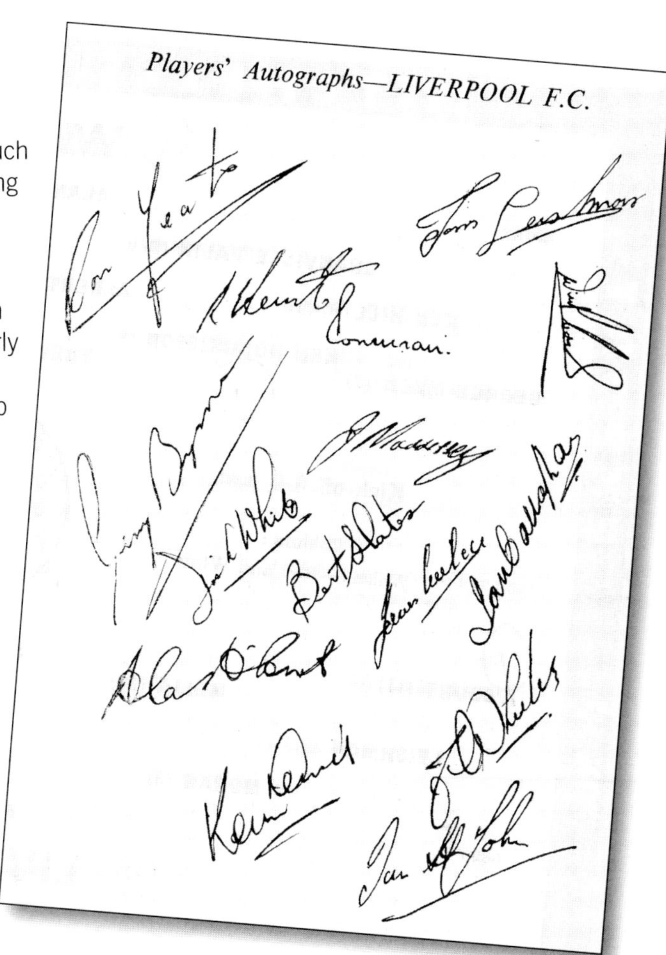

ROBERT SLATER
Goalkeeper
Scottish "B" International. Very much a line goalkeeper, being small in stature, and only 5ft 8 inches tall .He relies on his co-defenders to deal with the crosses, particularly centre-half Ron Yeats. However he makes up for his lack of inches with tremendous agility.

DICK WHITE
Full-back
In his eighth season at the club, having been signed from Scunthorpe United. His preferred position is centre-half, but with the arrival of Ron Yeats has now settled in the team as, a no nonsense, defensive full-back.

GERRY BYRNE
Full-back
Signed for the club at 17. Tough tackling, no nonsense player nicknamed "Gerry the Crunch". Shankly described him as the toughest player he had ever seen, mainly because of his bravery and recovery after sustaining injuries. He however is not a dirty player and in-fact has only been booked once. And that was for querying a throw-in!

GORDON MILNE
Wing-half
When Bill Shankly's became manager, Gordon was one of his first signings arriving from Preston North End in August 1960 for what was then a club record fee of £16,000. He reads the game well, anticipating the opposition's method of play. His accurate passing, coupled with the desire to get forward and support the attack for moves he has initiated make him a very polished performer.

RON YEATS
Centre – half
Signed for the club by Bill Shankly in July 1961 from Dundee United for £30,000, who described him as a colossus and promptly made him captain. He is 6 feet 2 inches tall and weighs 14 stone and the cornerstone of the defence.

TOMMY LEISHMAN
Wing-half
Signed from St Mirren in 1959. Good ball winner both on the ground and in the air. He also had a quick burst of speed, which would leave defenders struggling in his wake.

KEVIN LEWIS
Outside-right; 81apps 44 goals
Lanky winger signed from Sheffield United in 1960 for £13,000. Versatile player who can also play centre-forward, scoring goals regularly and often the spectacular with his thunderous shooting. Finished the clubs top scorer last season with 19 goals in 32 games. He is quick, skilful and good in the air, but also inclined to be unpredictable.

IAN St JOHN
Centre-forward
Signed for the club by Bill Shankly in May 1961 from Motherwell for £37,500, a club record at the time. Although primarily a striker and scores more than his fair share of goals, he also operates as a scheming inside-forward setting up chances for his team mates.

ROGER HUNT
Inside-forward
A prolific goal-scorer for the side in and around the penalty box, very strong and athletic and possessing great stamina, which allows him to cover the ground with ease, giving the defenders little time to settle.

JIMMY MELIA
Inside-forward
Local lad who joined the groundstaff at 15, and by the end of 1955 was in the first team. He is the play- maker for the team, scheming and setting up chances for his team-mates and also contributing more than his fair share of goals for the team.

ALAN A'COURT
Outside-left; 382 apps 63 goals
Combines speed on the flanks with great crossing ability and also packs a powerful shot. Alan has been capped for England five times and was selected for the 1958 World Cup Finals in Sweden, playing against Brazil, Austria and USSR.

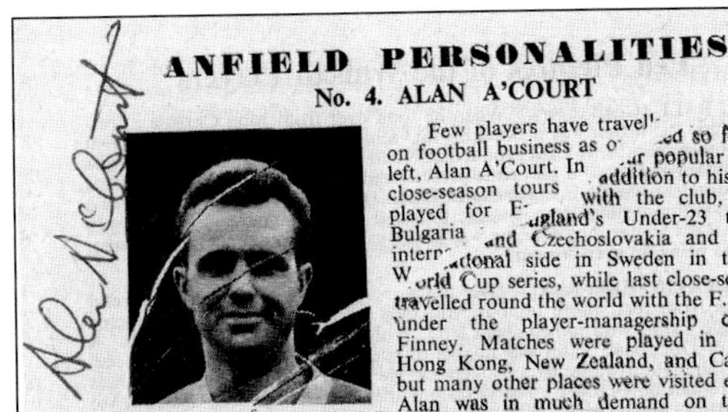

ANFIELD PERSONALITIES

No. 4. ALAN A'COURT

Few players have travelled so far afield on football business as our popular outside-left, Alan A'Court. In addition to his various close-season tours with the club, he has played for England's Under-23 team in Bulgaria and Czechoslovakia and the full international side in Sweden in the 1958 World Cup series, while last close-season he travelled round the world with the F.A. team, under the player-managership of Tom Finney. Matches were played in Malaya, Hong Kong, New Zealand, and California, but many other places were visited en route. Alan was in much demand on this trip, along with a few other members of the party, for coaching and lecturing to schools and youth clubs.

Alan first signed professional forms for us in September 1952, after a short spell as an amateur. Previously he had played in junior football in the Prescot area. He made his League debut on February 7, 1953, got his first Under-23 honour in 1956, and his first full England cap the following season. In all he has played in seven Under-23 games and five full internationals, and has appeared in 301 Football League games for the club, scoring 59 goals. On top of that he has played in 20 F.A. Cup-ties and numerous other matches.

Photo by courtesy of "Liverpool Echo"

ALF ARROWSMITH
Centre-forward
Popular 18 year old Mancunian youngster, who shows a good turn of speed, which coupled with his strength unnerves the best of defences. Typical 'Johnny on the spot', but also scores spectacular goals when least expected. A capable stand-in for St John.

IAN CALLAGHAN
Outside-right
Born Liverpool, signed as an apprentice, making his debut aged 17 years last season. An orthodox winger beating defenders with skill and able then to cross with uncanny accuracy making many goals for his team-mates.

JOHN MOLINEUX
Full-back
Signed in 1955, a defensive minded full-back and very strong in the tackle, lost his place to Dick White.

RONNIE MORAN
Full-back
Joined the club in 1952 as a 17 year old, a hard uncompromising left back. He was first team choice until this season when replaced by Gerry Byrne.

PEN PICTURES of the WALSALL team

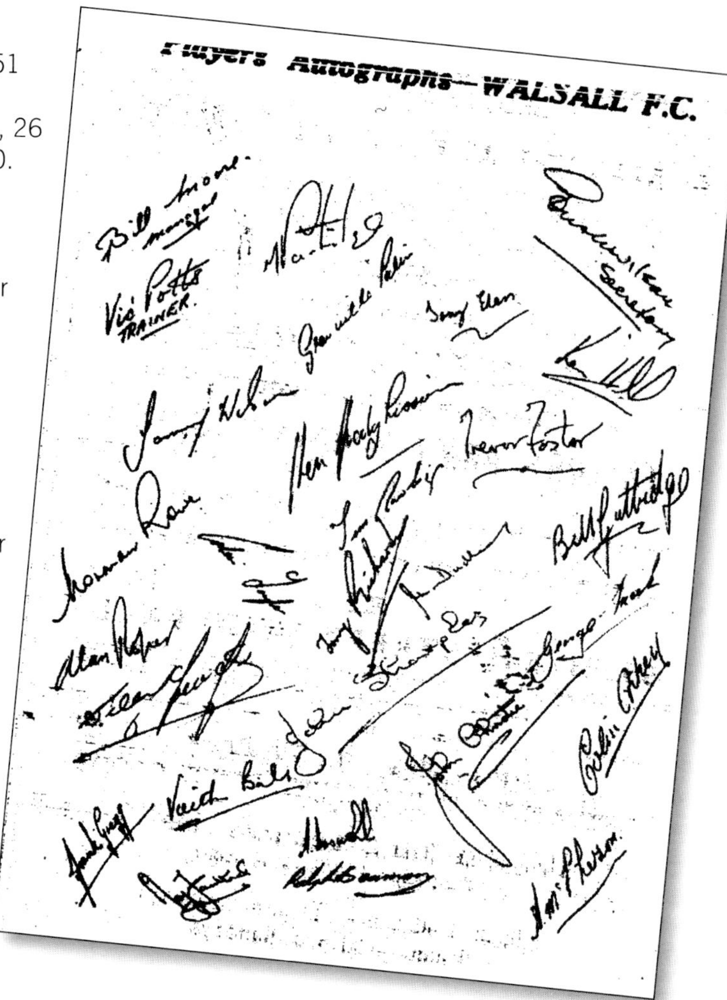

KEITH BALL
Goalkeeper; 51 apps.
Born: Walsall, 26 October 1940.
A local lad joining the club initially as an amateur in 1957, becoming a full time professional in July 1960. He was the dependable understudy for John Christie but came into the team two games prior to the Liverpool game. He was a solid, competent and brave keeper and an excellent shot stopper.

GRENVILLE PALIN
Full-back; 139 apps, 10 goals.
Born: Doncaster, 13 February 1940.
Previous club Wolverhampton Wanderers where he signed as a professional in 1957, but suffered a broken leg without having played for the first team. He was transferred to Walsall in July 1960 and helped the Saddlers win promotion to the Second Division. He made his debut at centre-half, but after one appearance

was switched to full-back. Tough tackling, no nonsense player, who liked to get forward and get the occasional goal.

JOHN SHARPLES
Full-back; 132 apps, 1 goal.
Born: Wolverhampton, 8 August 1934.
He joined Walsall from Aston Villa in August 1959 for whom he made 13 League appearances. He was a rugged and strongly built player who read the game well. Versatile player who was happy in either full-back postion and could also play centre-half if needed.

ALBERT McPHERSON
Centre-half; 367 apps, 8 goals.
Born: Salford, Manchester, 8 July 1927.
Previous club was Bury for whom he signed professional in1949, and spent three seasons before dropping out of the big time and joined Cheshire League side, Stalybridge Celtic. He joined Walsall in May 1954 and proved to be the kingpin and mainstay of the defence, being resilient, a good header of the ball and giving remarkably consistent performances throughout the successive promotions in 1960 and 1961. Little wonder then that he was also the captain of the team. He was also a mild mannered man for a big fella, which helped him get his point across.

KEN HILL
Wing-half; 141 apps, 1 goal.
Born:Walsall, 28 April 1938.
Joined Walsall as a professional in October 1956. Originally he came into the team as a right-back, but then became a hard working right-half, who would stick to his opponents like glue, covering every blade of grass. He established himself in the team that won promotion from Division 3.

JIMMY DUDLEY
Wing-half; 176 apps, 3 goals.
Born: Gartosh, Lanarkshire, 24 August 1928
He played for West Bromwich Albion, becoming a professional in 1945 on his 17th birthday and playing a total of 320 apps. He won a FA Cup winner's medal and a Scotland 'B' cap in 1954. Transferred to Walsall in December 1959 for a bargain fee of £4,000. His experience in a higher class of football has stood the club in good stead helping them to win successive promotions in 1960 and 1961. He was a very classy and eye catching wing-half, skilful and silky on the ball, and delivering the killer pass.

GEORGE MEEK
Winger; 187 apps, 29 goals.
Born Glasgow, 15 February 1934.
Diminutive Scot, who began his career at Hamilton Academical, before Major Frank Buckley took 5ft 3ins George as a professional to Leeds United in August 1952 where he made over 200 appearances scoring 19 goals and also playing alongside the legendary John Charles. He was loaned to Walsall for 15 months, whilst doing his National Service in 1954/55 and made 44 league appearances in a struggling Third Division South side and left a lasting impression with his fast direct play, good control and capable of playing on either wing and crossing the ball whilst on the run. Subsequently at the start of Season 1961/62 he was signed from Leicester City for a fee of £8,000, being the only new player from the team that clinched promotion from Division 3.

KEN HODGKISSON
Inside –forward; 352 apps, 56 goals.
Born: West Bromwich, 12 March 1933.
Joined Walsall from West Bromwich Albion in December 1955 for £1,600. He had been unable to break into the "Albion" first team due to internationals Ronnie Allen and Johnny Nicholls being at the club at that time. He was a skilful and scheming inside forward who also possessed a fierce shot, enabling him to chip in with his fair share of goals. A very influential player for the "Saddlers" in their glory years.

TOMMY WILSON
Centre-forward; 57 apps, 19 goals.
Born: Beddlington, County Durham, 15 September 1930.
He signed as a professional for Nottingham Forest in April 1951. Originally an outside-right, before switching to centre-forward with great success scoring 89 goals for Forest in 217 games (shades of the great Tom Finney, another hero of mine). In 1959 he won an FA Cup winner's medal before transferring to Walsall in November 1960 and helped them win promotion from Division 3. A very talented and scheming centre-forward, who also chipped in with a fair share of goals, showing good control with neat passes and the perfect foil for strike partner Tony Richards.

TONY RICHARDS
Centre-forward; 358 apps, 198 goals.
Born: Smethwick, 6 March 1934.
Tony's first club was Birmingham City, for whom he became a professional in 1951. His career was interrupted by National Service. After being demobbed he decided to write to the then manager of Walsall, Major Frank Buckley for a

trial and duly impressed and signed in September 1954. Leading the attack in successive promotion seasons, he has been top scorer for the club. Goalscoring comes naturally for this Johnny on the spot, with most of his goals coming in the penalty area, where he was fearless and not afraid of getting hurt even if it meant a diving header. Consistently the clubs leading goalscorer for the fourth successive season and the sixth all told, during which he has also beaten the long-standing club record of 165 goals by Gilbert Alsop

COLIN TAYLOR
Outside-left; 502 apps, 189 goals.
Born: Stourbridge, 24 August 1940.
Joined Walsall in February 1958 and quickly became a firm favourite with the fans due to his 'cannonball' shooting, which ensured more than it's fair share of spectacular goals, scoring 33 goals in season 1960-61 from the left wing, this also being the fourth season in succession that he has recorded double figures. One of the most dangerous wingers in the country, he has good control, possessing a wonderful left foot which unleashed his 'cannonballs', causing havoc amongst the defenders, particularly his hard low crosses.

JOHN CHRISTIE
Goalkeeper; 107 apps.
Born: Fraserburgh, 26 September 1929.
John started his career with Ayr United in 1946 before joining Southampton in 1951 for whom he played over 200 games before transferring to Walsall in June 1959 and subsequently helping the Saddlers win promotion from Divisions Four and Three in successive seasons. A safe and confident line goalkeeper, who's acrobatic saves often made the difference in close games.

COLIN ASKEY
Outside-right; 88 apps, 12 goals.
Born: Milton, Stoke-on-Trent, 3 October 1932.
Colin started his career with Port Vale in 1949, making 200 appearances and scoring 23 goals and helping them win the Third Division North championship in 1953-54. He joined Walsall on a free transfer in July 1958, helping the Saddlers clinch the Fourth Division title and scoring the memorable winning goal at Shrewsbury that clinched promotion to Division Two on Wednesday, April 26th, 1961. A fast raiding skilful direct winger giving the Saddlers good balance on the right flank, but recently replaced by George Meek.

BILL GUTTRIDGE
Full-back; 210 apps.
Born: Darlaston, 4 March 1931.
He signed as a professional for Wolverhampton Wanderers in 1948, transferring to Walsall in November 1954, after failing to establish his career there. He subsequently helped the Saddlers to achieve successive promotions in 1959-60 and 1960-61. Known affectionately as 'Chopper', due to his tough-tackling, no nonsense approach to the full-back position for which he could be a little over zealous at times.

BILL YOUNGER
Inside-forward; 8 apps, 5 goals.
Born: Newcastle-on-Tyne
Not many appearances for the Saddlers, but joined at the beginning of first ever season in Division Two. A classy inside-forward, with good control and possessing a powerful shot to his game.

The teams took to the field with the following line-ups,

Liverpool F.C

Slater 1

White 2 Byrne 3

Milne 4 Yeats 5 Leishman 6

Lewis 7 Hunt 8 St. John 9 Melia 10 A'Court 11

0

Taylor 11 Richards 10 Wilson 9 Hodgkisson 8 Meek 7

Dudley 6 McPherson 5 Hill 4

Sharples 3 Palin 2

Ball 1

Walsall F.C

Referee: Mr A. W. Luty (Leeds)

As you can see from how the teams lined up, it is a little strange to all the sophisticated variations to team play of the current era: It consisted of a Goalkeeper; a king pin defensive Centre-half (No 5); two defensive Full-backs (No 2 & No 3), who never ventured over the half-way line; two Wing-half's (No 4 & No 6), who alternated between defence and attack; two Inside-forwards (No 8 & No 10, one usually would be more attack minded, the other more of a schemer who could also chip in with his fair share of goals; two Wingers (No 7 & No 11) on the flanks feeding the crosses to provide the ammunition for his attacking team-mates and to cause havoc for the opposing defenders; and finally a Centre-forward (No

9) who would operate in the narrow track down the middle of the field, rarely crossing into his teams defensive half of the field.

The following report, has been taken from the Saturday evening edition of the Birmingham 'Sports Final',by reporter Frank Pemberton.

This was Walsall's first visit to Anfield for a league match since the 1893-94 season when Liverpool beat them there 3-0. Since then their paths had not crossed except in the 1947 F.A. Cup competition when Liverpool won 5-2 at Walsall.

Strange as it may sound Walsall, were one of the first members of the Second Division in 1892, whereas Liverpool did not join the league until a year later. Walsall, were then known as Walsall Swifts.

Heavy Pressure

Liverpool where in their customary red shirts and white shorts attacking the Kop end whilst Walsall were in their changed strip of blue shirts and white shorts and kicked off.

A neat dribble by Meek raised Walsall's hopes but his pass to the right, saw Richards who had moved out there dally and be dispossessed.

In the next minute Hunt had a glorious chance to put Liverpool ahead, he received the ball from a A'Court cross, but he too was slow in moving to the ball and Ball saved the situation by dashing out to the edge of the penalty area. There Hunt took a second shot but Ball was too close and the ball struck him.

Walsall's goal continued to have narrow escapes. One attack followed another with Liverpool dictating the course of play. They gained at least half a dozen corners in the first ten minutes and such was Liverpool's pressure that there was a period when Slater stood alone in the Liverpool half.

Meek was unlucky when receiving from Hodgkisson he fired in a shot that struck an opponent's head and sailed over the bar. Walsall however had to defend desperately against a very breezy Liverpool attack for some time.

Then, in the 23rd minute, after the home side had done so much attacking, Walsall took the lead. Taylor was sent away down the visitor's left and his jet propelled centre struck centre-half **Yeats** off whom it shot into the net like a bullet. This was the first time this season that Liverpool had been behind in a home league match.

Only a minute earlier Walsall's goal had an amazing escape when Hunt lifted the ball over the bar from only a couple of yards out.

Gradually, however, Walsall, who had defended magnificently, began to show their ability as attackers. Both wingers were prominent with Taylor the more dangerous. Another of the left-winger's crosses struck an opponent but this time the ball went wide of the goal for an un-productive corner.

When Melia stabbed the ball into the goalmouth Sharples shrewdly put it over his own goal-line for a corner that was well cleared.

Hunt was unlucky with a header that missed the crossbar by the merest of margins.

Yes, it was nearly all Liverpool, but praise this Walsall defence for a gallant performance, which at times deserved the luck that came their way.

Twice the ball was put into the visitor's net, but on each occasion the referee quite rightly ruled the player offside. The crowd which must have been in the region of 50,000, roared and roared as repeatedly Liverpool's attack moved menacingly on the Walsall goal.....a roar that once turned into a cheer when Ball saved a certain goal by diving at the feet of Melia just as the Liverpool man drove in with great force.

Ball with outstretched hands managed to turn aside for yet another Liverpool corner.

In the 41st minute Liverpool drew level with a goal by **Lewis** who received a short pass across the goal face from Hunt, who had received a through ball from Melia. Several times the referee had pulled Liverpool up for being offside when there was a doubt about it. This time, in my view, Hunt was yards offside when a Liverpool player pushed the ball forward to him.

Half-time Liverpool 1
Walsall 1

Two minutes after the resumption this speedy Liverpool attack moved into action. There seemed a grim determination about the work of **Melia** as he took the ball down the left wing, slipped it forward to Hunt-a glorious long pass-and the inside right, in the role of left winger, took the ball to the goal line, ran in and then passed back to Melia who drove it into the far corner of the net. It was a good move that produced a good goal.

Three minutes later McPherson let **Hunt** through to beat Ball from close range. This slip by McPherson was unfortunate for throughout a gruelling first half he had indeed played the part of captain courageous. That Liverpool on the play, were deserving their lead there could be no question.

Their movements were quick and well executed and it was quite easy to understand why they were at the top of the Second Division table.

Almost one way

For some time it had been virtually one- way traffic, towards the Walsall goal. Palin decided to transfer the play by a long ball up the right, but he was halted at the edge of the penalty area. His temporary wandering however, indirectly cost Walsall a goal, for in the 57th minute Melia, who was as great in defence as attack, cleared Palin's effort and a long ball downfield found **Hunt** in a wide open space. McPherson almost alone was powerless and in ran Hunt to score with ease.

Another four minutes of Liverpool attacking-and then their fifth goal. Once more Melia provided the opening, this time for **St. John** to tap the ball into the net.

In the 73rd minute Walsall's goal suffered a heavy bombardment in which the ball was kicked off the line and then driven back to crash against an upright.

Richards came into the picture with a shot that was a shade wide.

In the 80th minute Liverpool rubbed it in still further. A long centre from the right was headed in by St. John, Ball punched out, but the ball bounced at the feet of **Hunt**, who only had to stroke it into the net.

Official Attendance: 42,229.

Goals at a glance
23 minutes Liverpool 0, Walsall 1, Yeats (o.g.).
41 minutes Liverpool 1, Walsall 1, Lewis.
47 minutes Liverpool 2, Walsall 1, Melia.
50 minutes Liverpool 3, Walsall 1, Hunt.
57 minutes Liverpool 4, Walsall 1, Hunt.
61 minutes Liverpool 5, Walsall 1, St. John.
80 minutes Liverpool 6, Walsall 1, Hunt.

Liverpool's triumph over Walsall, recaptured by the camera, starts with Lewis (No. 7) turning Hunt's cross past Ball (Walsall) for goal No. 1. Below, Hunt gives Ball no chance to prevent the third goal.

Hunt cleverly sends Ball one way and shoots the other and the fourth goal is on the way to the net; and below, St. John enters the scoring lists by directing a Melia pass past the fallen goalkeeper.

Keith Ball

In summary my main recollections of the game are that Walsall's defence played magnificently during the first half against the slickest attack in the second division, who showed bewildering interplay between a first rate marksman in Roger Hunt and two top rate schemers in Jimmy Melia and Ian St. John, ably supported by the speedy wing play and promptings of Alan A'Court. Not many sides could have stopped this brilliant Liverpool attack. It had been a fantastic game, with Walsall taking the lead through a typical left wing cross from Colin (Cannonball) Taylor striking that big colossus of a centre half Ron Yeats, off whom it shot into the net like a bullet, he simply couldn't get out of the way. A wonderful moment, you go delirious, and the home crowd are silent. The brilliance of young goalkeeper Keith Ball and the dominance of centre half Albert McPherson kept the league leaders out until the 41st minute.

Jimmy Melia

However, deep down you knew they could not hold out in the second half if this sort of ferocity of attacking play continued and sure enough Walsall were ruthlessly swept aside, as the Merseysiders rapped home five goals in a 20 minutes spell of superb attacking football. Just to complete Walsall's unhappy day, they learned after the match that outside right George Meek had sustained a broken nose- the result of a collision with left back Byrne late in the game.

We had our moments in the game, taking the lead, when even the Liverpool supporters, standing behind us were stunned into disbelief, however subsequently every time a Liverpool goal was scored thereafter, they would tap my shoulder and say that's one, with this humiliation continuing until goal number six. This was probably one of the

worst experiences as a fan, even at this early age during that amazing 20 minutes spell, when it seemed only goalkeeper Keith Ball, stood between us and total humiliation. He stood no chance with the shots that beat him and it was his courage that kept the score down to six. He had been keen alert and dangerously daring and Walsall's man of the match. The man of the match overall had to be Liverpool's Jimmy Melia, he was in top class form with his quick thinking football brain causing havoc for the defenders and he was the schemer behind the avalanche scoring one goal and creating another three, not to mention being involved in all that was best in his teams play.

At the final whistle, even-though Walsall had been walloped, nothing had changed in relation to our support for our heroes, and far from feeling demoralised still realised they would still hold their own in Division Two, because we had just witnessed an outstanding performance by Liverpool, who come the end of the season would become installed as champions, with Walsall finishing in a respectable 14th position.

8.3.62

FOOTBALL LEAGUE
SECOND DIVISION

	P.	W.	D.	L.	F.	A.	Pts.
LIVERPOOL	29	20	4	5	72	27	44
LEYTON O.	30	17	5	8	56	32	39
PLYMOUTH	31	15	7	9	57	52	37
SCUNTHORPE	30	15	6	9	66	49	36
ROTHERHAM	29	14	7	8	59	51	35
SOUTHAMPTON	31	14	7	10	57	44	35
SUNDERLAND	30	14	6	10	58	42	34
STOKE	30	13	6	11	43	37	32
DERBY	30	12	7	11	56	54	31
LUTON	30	13	3	14	56	56	29
WALSALL	**29**	**11**	**7**	**11**	**48**	**51**	**29**
PRESTON	30	11	6	13	38	42	28
HUDDERSFIELD	28	9	9	10	42	41	27
NORWICH	30	10	7	13	45	58	27
NEWCASTLE	30	9	8	13	48	43	26
SWANSEA	30	9	8	13	45	66	26
BURY	29	11	2	16	36	60	24
BRIGHTON	30	7	10	13	30	58	24
BRISTOL ROVERS	30	10	3	17	39	57	23
CHARLTON	27	8	6	13	43	50	22
MIDDLESBROUGH	29	8	6	15	51	60	22
LEEDS	30	8	6	16	36	51	22

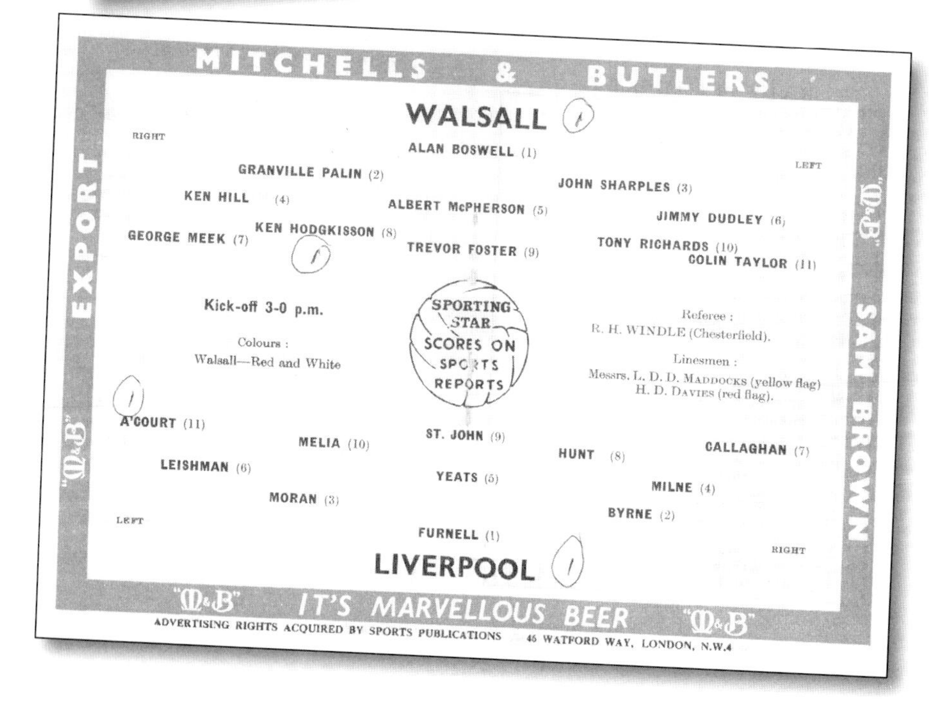

Liverpool had been awesome on the day, particularly in the second half and most other teams would have been overwhelmed.

Indeed in the return fixture on March 8th 1962 at Fellows Park, Walsall did in-fact earn a very creditable 1-1 draw. Liverpool having taken the lead rather fortuitously thanks largely to a mistake by the referee, who must have been unsighted after missing goalkeeper Alan Boswell being impeded on a right wing corner after 55 minutes, resulting in the loose ball being whipped into the net by Alan A'Court. Justice was done on 76 minutes when Walsall equalised through Ken Hodgkisson. The ball was crossed over from the left by Colin Taylor, headed down by George Meek into the path of "Hodgy", who rifled an unstoppable shot past debutant Liverpool goalkeeper Jim Furnell, who until then had repeatedly thwarted Walsall's attacks.

Chapter Seven

HOMEWARD BOUND

Tubby and I, went straight to Mrs Metcalfe's after the game and after a brief exchange of pleasantries and thank-you, we duly collected our bikes. She said, "Tara lads, look after yourselves, and god bless". It was around five o'clock when we left and still good day-light, so we didn't hang about knowing we had to get back in the saddle and start pedalling like mad to arrive home before midnight. Little did we know what was in store for us, on what was to be an eventful ride back home.

We had only cycled approximately 15 miles along the A 57, heading along the main highway into Warrington, with our backs already beginning to ache, so with very little traffic about we decided a little bit of riding no handed was the order of the day. Suddenly appearing from no-where on the other side of the road with its lights flashing at the front and a 'Dring dring, dring' from it's bells there was a black MG 'A' 1600 hard top sports police car, which proceeded to screech to a halt and do a 'U' turn on the highway, pulling up along side us as we cycled along. What's the dickens is this all about we thought as it proceeded to flag us down and one of the two police officers in the car jumped out, and beckoned us to get off our bikes.

When the police car came to a halt the police officer approached us, with a clipboard in his hand, and was quickly joined by his other colleague and the conversation went some-thing like this:

POLICEMAN "Where are you going lads?"

"Walsall" we replied.

POLICEMAN With a disbelieving look he said "Walsall, go on pull the other leg".

"Yes, we've been to the football, to see them play Liverpool at Anfield, and we are now on our way back home".

POLICEMAN Still looking some-what bemused the officer then said,

"Lad's, do you realise you are riding no handed on the main highway and that it is dangerous and could cause an accident".

"Sorry officer, but our backs are aching and we have just been having a little rest as we cycle along."

POLICEMAN "Give us your names and addresses lads, I will be reporting you both to the Chief Constable of Lancashire for riding on the main highway in a dangerous manner."

Gob smacked, I said "Will we have to come all the way back to Lancashire to answer the charge".

POLICEMAN "Probably, but it will be up to the Chief Constable to make the final decision".

He then cautioned us both and told us to be on our way and cycle more safely.

Worried sick Tubby and I began to think what on earth our parents would have to say when we got back home, and how this incident had marred our great adventure.

This delay meant it would soon be dusk, so we began to pedal in earnest heading out of Warrington on the A 50 towards Knutsford. It got darker and the cold autumn air was very noticeable around our faces as we continued through Knutsford, and onto Holmes Chapel when we were faced with another dilemma regarding the lights on our bikes. Because we had to use them early in the morning, some batteries had gone flat. Tubby now had a front light, but no rear light. I had a rear light, but no front light so we decided that Tubby would lead the way, with myself taking up the rear. Good thinking eh! It was also a little spooky as we cycled the road with open fields surrounding us.

It was around 9 o'clock when we reached Holmes Chapel and decided to stop at the George and Dragon public house, which is still owned by Robinson's Brewery of Stockport, albeit the pub has been refurbished in recent years. Here we spent our last amount of money, which was a combined two shillings (10 new pence) and bought a bottle of pop and a packet of crisps between us.

Feeling revived we resumed our journey. Heading along the open road, which by now was quite dark, and with only the light from the front cycle lamp, plus the headlights of passing vehicles to guide us on our way, It wasn't long before we encountered fog, reducing visibility and making it very tiring on our eyes and rather dangerous to proceed at the current speed.

As we approached the built up areas around Stoke, we began to tire rapidly, but kept our spirits up with continual banter, mostly with regards to how we were both feeling, plus the street lighting gave us added encouragement, and we even managed to spot two policemen patrolling on foot through the fog, but this time there was to be no altercation with the law. I knew Tubby was almost totally exhausted, however, but I did not relay to him that I felt likewise. Eventually, though the inevitable happened having just passed Stone and heading on towards Stafford, Tubby said "That's me finished, I've had it!" and collapsed into a ditch at the side of the road, taking his bike with him. Needing little encouragement I collapsed into the ditch also.

The time was around midnight, and the fog was a little thicker. We decided to have a sleep in the ditch to recharge our energies before the final push to get home. By now the cold had really got to us, but the saving grace was to be our yellow cycle capes, which we duly put one on the damp ground to lie on and the other over us to keep warm. Tubby also came up with the idea to push a yellow duster down our trousers to keep our nether regions warm. As we dozed in the ditch, near to an electricity pylon our sleep was constantly interrupted with the electricity crackling on the overhead power cables in the damp air, and the continual roar of Coaches belonging to Central and Dawson's of Walsall taking people home from the game, after they had taken in the Blackpool Illuminations. It really did hit us hard at the time, as we read the writing on the back of the coaches, we said wouldn't it be great if one of the coaches stopped and allowed us to put our bikes in the luggage compartment and also offered us a lift home. It was all wishful thinking as we huddled together in the ditch wet and cold. After spending a couple of hours in the ditch we decided on a last push for home.

The cold had now began to get a grip of us, so we kept the capes on, but our hands were freezing, and I remembered on passing through Stafford another little brainwave kept us going. Close to the old British Reinforced Concrete works on the A 34, where it crosses the main London West Coast railway line, there is a telephone box, so we stopped and both got inside for a warm, with particular attention for our hands, by way of the electric light bulb. Yes it was very innovative, but it certainly did the trick and needless to say encouraged us to complete the final hurdle to get home.

We were both now extremely dirty and dishevelled because of the fog and lying in ditches when we got to Tubby's house with the front door wide open, because his parents were wondering where the hell he had got to and were out looking; they had even sent his brother out searching the streets in his car, they hadn't a clue what he had been up to. I knocked the front door to be greeted, with great relief by my mother. We went into the kitchen for a cup of tea and noticed the kitchen clock showing half past four in the morning. Remember there were no mobile phones in those days, and most families couldn't afford phones, so it was a case of us showing up, albeit after being out for 23 hours and it was now Sunday morning.

So it was off to bed, to get around four hours sleep and ask my mother to get me up at half nine in the morning, so that I could cycle to Walsall in time to report for duty at half ten on the Lloyds Bank steps on the Bridge, to sell the Sunday newspapers. This was a little job I had working for a Mr Degville and his son Kenny. They used to go for a drink when the New Inns pub which opened at midday in Park Street, and stay there until half two, then they would come out and I could go home. I was paid 15 shillings (75 new pence), and allowed to take home various newspapers and comics, which my mom and dad were grateful to receive.

Numerous different customers used to frequent the stall, and a lot were regular customers who had their order put to one side in a big newspaper bag. One such customer was Mr Paul Marsten, a reporter with the Birmingham Post and Sports Argus. When he arrived to collect his papers, Kenny said to him, "What do you make of him and his mate, they cycled all the way to Liverpool to see Walsall play yesterday". Ever the conscientious reporter that he obviously was, he put down his papers and out came his notebook and pencil and our tale was published in the Birmingham Post the following morning Monday, October 16th 1961 under the heading:

Walsall F.C. "Enthusiasts".

If Walsall FC, have two more enthusiastic supporters than Tony Davis (16yrs) of Warner Road, and his friend, Geoffrey Bevan (15yrs), of Clare Road, I should like to hear from them.

They arrived at their homes at Coalpool at 4.30 yesterday morning after cycling a total of 180 miles to see Walsall play Liverpool-and lose by six goals to one. Was it worth it ! "Oh. Yes" they said. "We enjoyed the ride, except when we had to ride through fog late on Saturday night".

At midnight, they settled down to sleep in a ditch at Stafford and continued their journey two hours later.

Paul Marsten.

Reporter.

And by the way, we never did hear anything from the Lancashire police!

Chapter Eight

MATCH OF THE DAY RECOLLECTIONS.

ALAN A'COURT

As seen from the enemy camp by ALAN A'COURT, Liverpool's outside left on the day and also in the return fixture at Fellows Park.

Alan A'Court (Outside-left)

What I can remember about the game against Walsall at Anfield, which as you know we won 6-1 was that Walsall became the first team to score first and be in front until the 41st minute that was since the season began. Although we won 6-1 your side never gave up and kept trying right to the end and it was bad luck your right winger Meek broke his nose because I felt he was a good little player.

As for the reverse game, which you know was a draw 1-1 the crowd got a little agitated with the referee as they thought your goalkeeper Alan Boswell was fouled before I scored. I also remember Ken Hodgkisson who I thought was a good professional. However with 'tongue in cheek', I thought your 13th man was 'The Laundry wall'. It was quite close to the goal line and being rather faster than most as a winger had visions of crossing the ball and then running into the wall. Thankfully I lived to survive another day, so this has to be 'Memorable Draw.

It was interesting to read about your cycling story. As well as being a good distance, those roads in those days were not the safest. I like you used to belong to the Youth Hostel Association and did a lot of cycling in my younger days, particularly going into Wales.

Alan made 382 appearances for Liverpool scoring 63 goals. He was a skilful left-winger combining speed on the flanks, with great crossing ability and packed a powerful shot. He was capped for England five times, scoring on his debut against Northern Ireland and playing in the 1958 World Cup against Brazil. Alan was also ever-present for Liverpool in season 1961-62 playing in all 42 games.

Match of the day recollections by Walsall skipper and centre-half, ALBERT McPHERSON

All the lads were geed up going to Anfield to face the might of Liverpool, in our encounter to such a powerful team namely Ian St John, Roger Hunt, Jimmy Melia in the forward line and centre-half Ron Yeats in defence and our first season in the 2nd Division.

Well I can tell you we all prepared ourselves as well as possible in those days leading up to that eventful day, defending corner kicks and free kicks against the presence of the tall Ron Yeats and stifling the dangers of their powerful forward line. On the positive side how we could get back at them, their weak points if they had any in such a formidable team.

I did not sleep very well that Friday night, and we all met at Fellows Park to travel by coach to Anfield, stopping en-route at the hotel at Holmes Chapel for our pre-match meal, steak to the requirements you wanted it done or poached eggs on toast and on the day I would say not digesting it very well.

Finally arriving at Liverpool's ground an hour before the kick- off passing plenty of Walsall supporters going to the match, having a look at the pitch to see if your football boots had the right requirement stud for the length of grass that was on the pitch, that done, into the dressing room and getting changed for the game with the adrenalin flowing.

Well as you know it was backs to the wall from the onset roared on by a 42,000 crowd and against the run of play we stunned the Liverpool supporters by taking the lead with a cross from Colin Taylor being deflected by Yeats into his own net, this saw Liverpool showing renowned pressure and getting frustrated by repeatedly being held up by getting flagged for offside. This saw us holding on until the 41st minute when another offside decision, this time a blatant one saw Roger Hunt yards offside, but this time the linesman who had been taking stick from the Liverpool supporters kept his flag down allowing left winger Alan A'Court to cross the ball for Lewis to come from the right and score, with myself and other defenders caught off-balance. I feel if we could have held that 0-1 lead up to the half-time, we may have given them problems but it was not to be and five more goals in the second half resulted in a 6-1 thrashing, if I may add I enjoyed being on the field with so many established players and playing on the Anfield pitch; good memories.

Obviously your memories are good also for you must have been keen to venture that far on cycles along with your pal, sorry the result would not help on your return home.

Best Wishes
Keith Ball

Match of the day recollections by
The Walsall Man of the Match goalkeeper KEITH BALL

It was only my third game in the second division and to play against the league leaders at twenty years of age was exciting. Manager Bill Moore's words were still ringing in my ears, "Just because you are now in the team, don't play about and do not be complacent and think you have made it!"

Playing against Roger Hunt, Ron Yeats, Jimmy Melia, Alan A'Court, Ian St John and others who were to become great players, was like a dream.

The game itself I recall seemed to be like the Alamo with attack after attack of red and white shirts coming at you.

A lot has been written about the crowd at Anfield, the atmosphere the crowd of

42,000 plus created was unbelievable, the noise they generated was deafening. I recall shouting something to Grenville Palin, who was maybe only a few yards away and he couldn't hear me. It was the biggest crowd that I played in front of and a great experience.

I remember women and youngsters in particular shouting and swearing at me when I retrieved the ball from behind the goal. (It didn't always end up in the back of the net that day). I heard someone shout at me, "Hey you have a nice arse there wack". In their scouse accent it was hilarious.

Like your own account of cycling to and from Anfield on that memorable day, it was a fantastic experience I cherish, one I will never forget.

Match of the day recollections by Walsall right-winger GEORGE MEEK

I can remember we had played okay in the first half, but after the interval things did not go very well. Liverpool, were well on top and there was only going to be one winner that day.

The one thing I can always remember was Ian St John broke my nose with his head. The other thing about that game when beaten by that score, it is a long way home. I must say not as long as your journey with your friend on bikes. On this form you could see why Liverpool at that time were expected to go up to the 1st Division.

As you can see George has certainly put the record straight with regards to how he came to break his nose during the game even-though it was 45 years after the event. The match report stated it was sustained as a result of a collision with left back Gerry Byrne late in the game.

Match of the day recollections by Walsall right-back GRENVILLE PALIN

Albert McPherson might not have slept very well the Friday night prior to the game, I certainly did not because I developed a nasty migraine attack and it was still causing me considerable distress on Saturday morning. When we arrived at the hotel in Holmes Chapel for our pre match meal en route to Liverpool I told manager Bill Moore that I was feeling unwell and not up for the game. He said that there was no one to take my place and that I would have to play, and suggested that I try drinking a couple of brandies. When we arrived at Anfield needless to say I was feeling much better and gave a creditable performance. I enjoyed the game even allowing for the result.

I never did ask Grenville if his migraine returned after the game, due to the defence having been subjected to such a second half run around, and whether it was the thought of facing the Liverpool attack on Friday evening that brought the migraine attack on in the first place. In those days there was only a twelfth man and no other reserves taken to away games along with the manager and trainer and usually two or three directors due to the expense.

Match of the day recollections by Walsall inside-forward KEN HODGKISSON

Ken's main recollection was very similar to that of Albert McPherson, he became very incensed with the decision given for Liverpool's equalising goal in the 41st minute. I thought Roger Hunt was blatantly offside and as we lined up for the restart I said to the referee "You've bloody well given them that goal!" He promptly booked me for dissent to the decision.

As I came out at the start of the second half with Jimmy Dudley, Ian St John trotted along side us and said "We'll score five more goals this half", and sure enough that's what happened in double quick time.

Best Wishes
Ken Hodgkisson

Chapter Nine

AND FINALLY:
THE WALSALL, LIVERPOOL CONNECTION.

The legendary Liverpool manager Bill Shankly was once quoted as saying : "Some people believe football is a matter of life and death, I am very disappointed with that attitude. I can assure you it is much, much more important than that".

However, in the 50's and 60's football was played in a more carefree manner, without the modern day pressures of tactics, and win at all costs mentality, plus the sponsorship and monetary rewards to clubs and players was not there.

This was illustrated to me when I met the great Sir Tom Finney, and told him that in 1957 I went to the Walsall Co-op in Bridge St to get Sir Stanley Matthews autograph, as he was promoting his football boots. Stanley said he had received a fee of £500, and asked Tom how much he was getting for promoting his boots, and was a little surprised to hear that he had negotiated his own deal, of so much for every pair sold. Tom had a business head because he owned his own plumbing business, and therefore secured the more lucrative deal. This type of deal would only be available to the top players of the day.

Walsall were a Cinderella club constantly having to apply for re-election until Bill Moore arrived and created this wonderful team, which has given me the inspiration to write about supporting the "Saddlers" during the greatest period in their history, and in particular in the story of the Liverpool bicycle ride, which always seemed to capture the imagination to those who heard the story.

In 1969, whilst on a coach tour holiday in Italy, my wife and I became friendly with a couple from Liverpool, and this has led us to go back and forth to the city to the present day. The bicycle ride plus the Liverpool friendship, should now show how my affection for Liverpool developed and has given me another team to support all these years, with the added bonus of both teams play in red, which is my preferred team colour anyway. However the first result I always look for is the "Saddlers".